18
Common
MISTAKES

S MALL BUSINESS O WNERS M AKE

by Nanci Appleman-Vassil, CSP
and Karen Parker

ISBN:0692756310
ISBN-13: 978-0692756317
Library of Congress Control Number: 2016919262
APLS Group, Raleigh, NC

Dedication

This book is dedicated to the memory of my father, Mitch Appleman: a man of large stature and presence who started his own business when other fathers were company men; whose kind heart and business sense gained him the devotion of his employees, associates, community and family; who provided me with unconditional love, guidance and support; and who taught my brother and me the value of turning our passions into successes.

I am proud to be his daughter, and I am forever grateful for his wisdom and encouragement that enabled me to follow in his entrepreneurial footsteps and launch APLS Group in 2000.

Acknowledgments

It truly takes a village to accomplish creating and publishing a book. I am thankful to the following people for being part of making this first *18 Common Mistakes* book a reality:

John Nicholas Vassil, my husband, business partner, and partner in life who contributed to this book by sharing his own successes and challenges of being a small business owner. Thank you for listening to my countless stories, fears, and concerns, and for helping grow APLS Group into the successful HR, Leadership, and Talent Development firm it is today.

Fred Jefferson, Director of Wake Technical Community College's Small Business Center, and Wayne Loots, retired Dean of Wake Technical Community College's Business and Industry Services, for asking me to create ten different topic titles that I could design and present to help small business owners. That was 14 years ago, and since then we have delivered to over 1000 current and future small business owners. My thanks to all the participants who came out on a Tuesday evening to attend the seminar and were willing to stretch, grow and share.

APLS Group team members Joy Drew for her red pen/eagle eye for editing, and Tina Valdecanas for her graphic design creativity and expertise.

And to my life-long friend, co-author, and business partner, Karen Parker: thank you for the countless hours of discussing this book, writing multiple drafts, re-writing the examples, suggestions, etc., which resulted in a product we both can be proud of.

September 2016

18 Common Mistakes
Small Business Owners Make

 Coach Nanci Says:

- Starting a successful business takes more than having a great idea.

- A great idea does not identify the skills, talent, and abilities needed to start a business.

- A great idea is the brainchild of the business, not the business itself.

- Action, planning, and implementation turn a great idea into a business.

- Cash management, budgets, and cash flow determine how well you prepare to turn the great idea into a viable business.

- A great idea needs professional assistance (accountant, banker, lawyer) to sustain a successful business.

- You create the infrastructure to change the great idea into a business.

Having a GREAT IDEA is Enough #1

Personal Experience

My husband, Nick, his best friend, Steve, and I opened a deli in Old Town Alexandria, VA. We decided not to hire an accountant because I had always been an ace with numbers. Eighteen months after opening the business, we got a call from the Internal Revenue Service about tax forms that were never filed. I thought because the group was not taking a salary, no forms had to be filed. I forgot I had written our partner, Steve, a few checks. The IRS had no tolerance for the mistake and charged the business $3000.

The deli experience proved that a great idea needs professional assistance. When I opened APLS Group, the first thing I invested in was a consultation with an accountant to learn what was required to open a business in the state of North Carolina. The accountant helped me set up the business with the proper infrastructure. She explained the pros and cons of opening the business as a corporation, sole proprietorship, partnership, LLC, or S corporation.

APLS Group is far more successful than my previous entrepreneurial effort because I learned that having a great idea is not enough to start and support a business. The original accountant provided business services that kept APLS Group solvent for many years. I smiled every time I wrote a check to her because the IRS was taken care of by a professional that left me free to run my business. She prepared the essential business documentation:

- Quarterly financial statements

- Quarterly tax forms

- Annual corporate tax return.

It is a good idea to periodically revisit your professional services providers to make sure that your growing needs match the services they provide. Your business growth may require additional professional services that are beyond the scope or price point of your original accountant, banker, or lawyer. Shopping around for an appropriate match between your business and a professional service provider is smart entrepreneurship.

Suggestions

- Research what you need to know and learn about it before you act on a great idea. Visit the U.S. Small Business Administration (SBA) at www.sba.gov.

- Read books, attend seminars, and watch webinars on what it takes to open, run, and manage a business. Visit SCORE at www. score.org for mentor, workshop, and library information.

- Create an operational plan. *The One Page Business Plan for the Creative Entrepreneur* by Jim Horan is an easy read for new business owners.

- Design a budget and cash management system.

- Hire an accountant, banker, business consultant, lawyer, and recruiter (not full-time employees).

- Hire the right personnel for your business.

 Coach Nanci Says:

- An important part of initial business planning is cash management.

- Lack of cash can shut down a business before it opens.

- Running a successful business requires sufficient cash to fund the business beyond start up.

- Adequate capital relieves the pressure of first-day revenue from a new business.

- Keeping the business open demands client revenue or ample cash reserves.

- Insufficient operating capital can inhibit a business from growing.

Lack of Cash   #2

Personal Experience

Providing training and consulting services is a great idea but a tricky business. As a consultant, it can easily take four to six months before an organization becomes a client. Although I opened APLS Group on July 1, 2000, the first revenue-generating business actually took place on November 8, 2000.

That first training session took place in a cold, unheated trailer; someone in the company had forgotten to turn on the heat. There was no warning nor mention of moving the training to a more conducive location. I did the training in a coat, scarf, and gloves because canceling was not an option. My focus was on delivering quality service to my first paying client.

It took four months to secure that paying client. My overhead was minimal because I ran the company from an office in my home and I was the only employee. Even though I had planned for six to eight months' worth of expenses for my start-up business, I had not projected an economic downturn where companies reduced their budgets for consulting services.

APLS Group survived three economic downturns in 2001, 2005, and 2009, when the US economy severely hurt small businesses. Revenues were down 35-55 percent because companies were delaying training and diminishing its purpose as a critical element for business survival. By 2011, I felt I had a handle on cash management of a small business.

I decided to seek assistance from the U.S. Small Business Administration (SBA) in the form of a loan to grow the business. I used the infusion of cash to initiate the following projects:

- Upgrade website
- Improve APLS Marketplace (online store)
- Enhance and renovate infrastructure
- Hire Team Project Manager.

Over fifteen years later, APLS Group has a reputation for providing excellent training and consulting services. If presented today with the situation from my first client, I would reschedule the training for a more appropriate location. I would be prepared to walk away from the client revenue if we could not agree to reschedule. I rely on APLS Group's reputation to generate income and I am unwilling to sacrifice quality for revenue.

Suggestions

- Start your business with a minimum of 4-6 months' income to cover business expenses. Discover the book *Small Time Operator: How to Start Your Business, Keep Your Books, Pay Your Taxes and Stay Out of Trouble* by Bernard B. Kamoroff, CPA, to help you with financially setting up your new business.

- Review funding ideas at StartupNation, www. startupnation.com.

- Include paying yourself in your cash flow management.

- Set realistic projections about incoming revenue.

- Track your expenses.

- Hire the appropriate people when you need them to do a job.

- Learn how to read a cash flow statement.

- Focus on cash flow, sales, and profits as part of your cash management strategy.

Coach Nanci Says:

- Running a successful business requires staying aware of the trends, peaks, and down times in your industry.

- Growing too fast tests the business's credibility.

- Planning for growth is an addendum to the original business plan.

- Inefficient development impacts the quality of the product or service.

- "Bigger" does not always translate into "better" customer service.

- Hasty expansion can be a threat to customer loyalty.

- Evaluate the return on investment before considering a growth spurt.

- Growing too fast can cause unnecessary chaos.

Growing Too Fast #3

Personal Experience

I once knew of a small company that created specialty bricks. The company produced three bricks a day that could be mailed out in 24 hours. In the early days, business was steady, and the owner had visions of expanding. Before he drew up a plan to increase production, the owner received an order on a Monday for 100 bricks to be delivered by the following Friday. He said "No problem" and accepted the order.

The owner thought that this would be his opportunity to expand, so he added two people to the staff to make the bricks. Due to time constraints, he didn't check references and believed that each new employee had previous brick-making experience. The owner soon discovered that there was a disparity in the quality of the completed bricks and that both workers did not produce bricks at the same pace. Even though working overtime was agreed upon at the interview, one of the new hires refused to work more than eight hours, regardless of additional pay for overtime.

Friday was coming to an end, but the order was incomplete. The owner tried to stall, but the customer insisted that the bricks be delivered that day. Since the company did not deliver the product that was promised, it took at least seven interactions before the customer trusted the company again to deliver any product. Customer loyalty is a casualty of this transaction.

Consumers are not loyal in today's market without proof that the business can provide the goods/services on time and at a competitive price. Your growing pains are not a customer concern, and an inability to meet customer demand will hurt your business's credibility.

At APLS Group, it is a core value to build a relationship with each customer. If we cannot accommodate a customer, we discuss alternatives or recommend trusted competitors who can meet the customer's needs. The loss of business is temporary, but the goodwill gained for helping a customer is long term. Our growth plan is to exceed customer expectation by providing consistent, superior customer service. The payoff is repeat business.

Suggestions

- Know what product or service your business produces.

- Be honest about what you can or cannot deliver in the agreed-upon time frame.

- Walk away if you cannot provide a quality service or product.

- Network with other business owners in your industry as resources for trends, marketing, and growth.

- Customer service is your lifeline. Remember to protect the relationship as your business expands.

- Develop a relationship with a few reliable competitors to use as referrals if you cannot accommodate a customer.

- You are looking for a sustainable customer base; support loyalty over the one-shot deal.

- Calculated expansion is more lucrative than fast growth.

 ## Coach Nanci Says:

- Ineffective interpersonal skills cause business owners to break all the rules of good management.

- Small business owners need effective interpersonal skills to hire the right people.

- A small business owner's lack of personal skills affects employee training and development.

- Ineffective interpersonal skills are responsible for poor relationships with clients.

- Repeat business and customer loyalty rely on sound interpersonal skills of the small business owner and the employees.

- A small business owner's poor interpersonal skills impede business growth.

Ineffective Interpersonal Skills #4

Personal Experience

A college friend shared the following work situation with me: The receptionist at her company is in the wrong position and the business owner refuses to give the employee feedback about her interpersonal style. Her interpersonal skills are poor and negatively affect business. The receptionist is rude to customers and to other employees. She shops on her computer instead of maintaining company reports. She leaves early or does not come in at all whenever someone else in her immediate work team has a scheduled day off. She argues with some customers and gossips with others, and she is the first to point out an error in another employee's work but takes no responsibility for errors in her own work.

The owner of the company rarely communicates directly with the employee and ignores the numerous complaints from co-workers and customers. The receptionist is a single mother and the owner feels she needs the job. Both employee and owner have ineffective interpersonal skills, and the business is suffering.

Suggestions

- The business owner might be the "idea person" but the wrong one to run the business.

- When hiring employees who will have direct customer contact, small business owners need to interview for effective interpersonal skills as well as technical skills.

- Nurture relationships with both customers and employees who are valuable to your business.

- Coaching employees is essential for development, retention, promotion, and profitability.

- Providing feedback to employees is an effective tool for a business owner.

 ## Coach Nanci Says:

- Lack of strategic planning results in poor decisions about the business you are creating.

- Incomplete strategic planning undermines finding initial capital to open the business because the business owner is inadequately prepared.

- When a strategic plan is poorly initiated, areas like hiring and running daily operations suffer.

- Inadequate strategic planning negatively impacts location, expansion, and inventory management.

- Effective marketing of your business depends on strong strategic planning.

Not Creating a Strategic Plan #5

Personal Experience

I knew a woman named Andrea who enjoyed being around children and pets. Andrea left her corporate job to open a business that provided in-home, short-term child care and pet care. She created a business plan and obtained a lawyer. Against legal advice, Andrea did not bother to secure financing because it was a home-based business with very low overhead. She immediately acquired clients by putting a small ad in a local neighborhood newspaper and listing the service on Craigslist. Her clients called in for the service, and she dispatched people to her customers' homes. Andrea's reputation for flexible, supportive service spread throughout the community.

Unfortunately, Andrea did not have a strategic plan to accommodate the immediate success of the business. She had more orders than she could fill alone or with the few additional service providers she had available. Andrea advertised for more service providers, but some of her choices were made out of haste instead of proper fit.

Andrea had a good idea but poor strategic business planning. After two years of working seven days a week as a service provider, administrator, and business owner, she closed her doors. Andrea gave up her dream of small business ownership and returned to the corporate world.

Suggestions

- Create a strategic business plan to accommodate your good idea.

- Seek the help of professionals (accountant, banker, lawyer) and take their advice.

- Determine what type of financing you need to start your business: savings, investors, Small Business Administration (SBA) loans, or bank loans, and include that information in your strategic plan.

- If you are borrowing from a bank or securing an SBA loan, you will need a strategic business plan. Initial financing will drive your strategic business plan.

- Women, if your business consists of a single product or service and does not require a loan, read the book *The One Page Business Plan for Women in Business* by Jim Horan and Tamara Monosoff to help you create your strategic plan.

- For an in-depth analysis of small business management, read the book *Effective Small Business Management* by Norman Scarborough, Thomas Zimmerer and Doug Wilson.

 Coach Nanci Says:

- Failing to innovate is a sign of complacency and a roadblock to success.

- Innovation is essential for business growth.

- Your employees are at a technological disadvantage and easy prey for competitors if you fail to innovate.

- Innovation helps your product or service become better, faster, and smarter.

- Innovation is shrewd business that attracts customers and makes your business stand out among competitors.

- Risk is inherent whether your business innovates or not.

Failing to Innovate

#6

Personal Experience

Training is people-intensive and has a history of face-to-face interaction to outline goals, learn new ways of operating for increased productivity, and follow up on action plans. The increased pressure to use technology in delivery of service while not sacrificing discussion and skill building is a challenge.

At APLS Group, innovation is the cornerstone of our business. We are constantly looking at what is trending in training and assessing how we can deliver substance and value to our clients.

In 2011, we delivered our first virtual Myers-Briggs Type Indicator® (MBTI®) with an international group in London. The MBTI is a personality inventory that uses the psychological types in Carl Jung's work to help people understand their preferences for operating in the world. We nicknamed the job our "Across-the-Pond Experience."

The MBTI is an interactive exercise, so we had to be creative about ways to collect and give information to the client. We customized the program for them and enlisted a person on-site in London to be our eyes for the implementation. We used technology wherever we could to complement the experience; this accommodated the digital natives in the work group.

Upon completion of the MBTI, we informed the client that this was our first time delivering the instrument remotely and we requested feedback. The client was impressed with the training and hired APLS Group for two additional training assignments.

Suggestions

- Challenge your comfort level. If you are comfortable with how you are doing business, you are behind the eight ball.

- Make innovation an integral part of your strategic business plan.

- Focus on technology trends for your product or service.

- Network with other business owners in your industry to share ideas and observe larger players to spotlight trends.

- Use social media to monitor the competition and to market your innovations.

- Stay ahead of the curve to ensure a cutting-edge business reputation in the marketplace by participating in webinars, attending seminars, and reading about trends. Pick up a copy of *The Next Big Thing: Spotting and Forecasting Consumer Trends for Profit* by William Higham.

- Engage your customers in casual conversation to determine the products/services they want, and use innovation to consistently target their needs.

Coach Nanci Says:

- Attempting to go it alone is the downfall of many small business owners.

- Know when and how to delegate. When the owner does everything, there is high potential for business failure.

- Single-mindedness sabotages a great idea and destroys the elements of the infrastructure.

- Attempting to go it alone ignores the three sets of skills needed to create small business success: technical, administrative, and institutional.

Attempting to Go It Alone

#7

Personal Experience

When I opened APLS Group, I was confident of my skills as a trainer/consultant. I spent many years in corporate business and was ready to be an independent. I liked the idea of having control of my client base and service delivery.

I learned from my previous business venture at the deli with my husband and Steve that seeking professional help from an accountant, a banker, and a lawyer was part of a small business strategic plan. I thought I could handle the minimal administrative duties myself since I had basic technology skills. The telephone and answering machine would suffice in the beginning until I could afford an employee or a service to handle incoming calls.

Once APLS Group arrived in the marketplace, it became apparent that clients were asking for services that required more sophisticated technical skills than I had anticipated.

In 2000, the internet, email, Microsoft XP, PowerPoint, and various Mac applications were beginning to dominate business technology. I found myself scrambling to find inexpensive administrative help with the technical skills necessary to keep my business operating and competitive.

I learned a few important lessons from this experience. Not only is securing professional services crucial to the success of a small business, but establishing the need for immediate personnel prior to opening is an essential strategic planning item. Attempting to go it alone took me away from building my client base. Had I recognized the need for administrative help from the beginning, I could have saved myself time, money, and business anxiety.

Suggestions

- Anticipate ancillary skills needed for business success in your strategic business plan that will complement your skills as an owner.

- Use outside consultants to provide constructive criticism of your business plan. They may see areas you have overlooked that could present a challenge.

- Consider adding partners with different skill sets.

  Develop clear expectations and establish contracts through your lawyer.

- Prepare to move the company from infancy to maturity with the appropriate people on board.

- Find out what type of mindset you are operating in by reading the book *Mindset: The New Psychology of Success* by Carol S. Dweck, Ph.D.

 Coach Nanci Says:

- Transparency in small businesses provides clarity among all parties involved in the success of the business: owner, staff, vendors, and customers.

- Ineffective communication sends mixed messages that interfere with the success of the business

- Poor communication between owner and employees has a negative effect on customers.

- Limited communication with unclear vision between owner and staff is often linked to inventory irregularities. (i.e., the left hand doesn't know what the right hand is doing).

- A major contributor to why employees leave an organization is absence of transparency.

Lack of Transparency

#8

Personal Experience

As a consultant, I have access to a wide variety of organizations and small businesses. The businesses that have open communication with owners/management and value employee input have a greater success rate in terms of profitability and retention. The effect of transparency in business is reflected in annual Best Places to Work lists provided by Forbes, Fortune, Glassdoor, and local business journals. The winners are traditionally high performers with impressive balance sheets.

My favorite Best Places to Work list comes from Glassdoor because the information reveals employees' internal impressions of their workplace. According to the online company overview, Glassdoor is a jobs and recruiting site that has a database of over 8 million company reviews, CEO approval ratings and employee interviews. In 2016, Mark Zuckerberg of Facebook, Jeff Weiner of LinkedIn, Sundar Pichai of Google, and Tim Cook of Apple topped the list of the most favorable CEOs. One reason linked to transparency included the weekly TGIF meetings at Google, where an open forum allows employees and executives to participate in an interactive question-and-answer session. Employees report that the executives are responsive no matter how difficult the questions. The meetings introduce new projects and keep employees in the loop.

Eventbrite, a self-service ticketing and events platform, has consistently scored high among small and medium-sized businesses in Glassdoor's Best Places to Work category. In an interview, one employee commented, "The leadership team is intentionally and remarkably transparent." Employees gave Eventbrite high marks for weekly question-and-answer sessions with the CEO and praised the company's use of feedback as a routine part of the developmental cycle.

Suggestions

- Listen, listen, listen—and then respond.

- Focus on good listening skills to provide a win/win result in communication with employees, customers, and vendors.

- Be a leader and a coach to employees.

- Provide employees with clear and consistent instruction and feedback.

- Offer opportunities for employees to be included in the big-picture vision you have for the business.

- Let your actions reflect the value your employees bring to the business, and encourage employee input to make the business better.

- Show customers they are valued by encouraging feedback about your products/services, and credit them when you implement forward-thinking ideas.

- Be transparent with vendors by communicating reasonable expectations for their services.

- Visit www.glassdoor.com to see the annual results of which organizations are the best and worst places to work, according to interviews with company employees.

 ## Coach Nanci Says:

- Overlooking your own strengths and developmental areas limits your business success.

- Recognizing your strengths can provide insight into what you know how to do and where your passion lies.

- Identifying your strengths gives value to your great idea and why you want to own a business.

- Self-awareness of developmental areas reveals your blindsides and your weaknesses.

- Understanding your developmental areas provides insight into how to staff your business.

- Realistic self-assessment helps a business owner remain grounded and in tune with the development of a profitable business.

Overlooking Your Own Strengths and Developmental Areas

#9

Personal Experience

One of my clients wanted APLS Group to help him develop a proposal for an international project. The client described what he wanted to accomplish through the project, and he even had a prospective client. However, he lacked a strategic plan, evidence of appropriate skill sets to implement the plan, and a strategy to take his idea to market.

The client could not provide us with enough concrete information to formulate a proposal. Before APLS Group could help him develop a proposal, we had to take him back to the beginning where we reviewed his idea and assessed his skill sets to see if he would be able to put all the necessary pieces together to move forward.

We wanted to be positive with the client and help him recognize that he was a visionary; this was his strength. He had a great idea but he did not have an implementation strategy. Proposal development was premature.

We proceeded to brainstorm the areas he needed to develop in order to move his idea from a vision to a reality. He went back to the drawing board confident about his strength as a visionary, clear about his skill sets, and aware of his developmental areas. The client appreciated APLS Group redirecting his initial request to accommodate his needs. He realized he was not ready for this particular international proposal, but he had the tools to put together a plan to move forward on future proposal development.

Suggestions

- Study your own strengths and weaknesses to determine if you're the right person to start a business.

- Conduct an online search for free assessments to determine your leadership style. Explore Mind Tools at www.mindtools.com.

- Go to a business coach/counselor or look online for a personality profile like DiSC® (www.aplsgroup.com, "Products") or the MBTI (www.myersbriggs.org).

- Take a course at a local community college on leadership and/or personality styles.

- Use your strengths to develop your business.

- Consider both strengths and developmental areas when writing your implementation plan. Seek support in your developmental areas to help structure your business. Visit BizFilings at www.bizfilings.com/toolkit for free downloads on small business information.

- Participate in a chat with small business owners on social media (e.g., LinkedIn) to get advice on what to expect when starting a new business.

 ## Coach Nanci Says:

- Feedback is a gift because the giver offers a perspective that may impact your business.

- A know-it-all business owner limits opportunities for a lucrative business.

- Seek feedback about operations and customer service to enhance your business.

- Do not be afraid to listen, assess, and respond to feedback from employees and customers.

- Establish a business climate where feedback is a positive experience for you, your customers, and your employees.

- Giving employees a voice gives them a reason to stay invested and help you grow your business.

Failing to Seek and Respond to Feedback #10

Personal Experience

Prior to opening my own business, I worked in two different organizations that had polar opposite views on feedback. I first became aware of the concept of feedback at NTL Institute, a non-profit training organization in Virginia. The company culture valued feedback both internally with staff and externally with clients. Leadership was open to hearing employees' thoughts and suggestions without retribution. The openness to feedback created an inclusive environment where employees felt that they continually contributed to the growth of the organization.

After 14 years at NTL, I moved to another company where feedback was used as a management tool to inform employees about their mistakes. "Feedback" consisted of one-way negative communication from a manager to an employee. During my employment with the company, I received feedback from two of my superiors by voicemail after hours. There was no opportunity for clarification or discussion. I considered the communication a reprimand, while management called it "feedback." Feedback as practiced in this environment was punitive and demotivating to employees, and it was an exclusive communication style reserved for management. The employees' observations and opinions were not welcomed.

Suggestions

- Cultivate relationships with your staff and customers because they have a vested interest in your success.

- Establish a company culture where there are no consequences for honesty about products or services.

- Meet with staff at regular intervals to seek feedback about what is working in the business and what needs improvement.

- Create an opportunity for customers to provide feedback on products and services.

- If you are unfamiliar with how to effectively use feedback to enhance your business, read the sage advice in the book *What Did You Say? The Art of Giving and Receiving Feedback* by Edith Seashore, Charlie Seashore, and Gerald Weinberg.

- To understand how to accept feedback without feeling insulted, pick up the book *Thanks for the Feedback: The Science and Art of Receiving Feedback Well* by Douglas Stone and Sheila Heen.

 # Coach Nanci Says:

I had to bring in a few experts to help with this one.

- Running a successful business requires mastery of the various challenges that occur in a timely manner (e.g., cash flow issues, incomplete product delivery, theft, inconsistent employees, customer complaints, and weather).

- "How soon 'not now' becomes 'never.'" (Martin Luther)

- "Procrastination is suicide on the installment plan." (Anonymous)

- "Tomorrow is often the busiest day of the week." (Spanish proverb)

- "Until you value yourself, you will not value your time. Until you value your time, you will not do anything with it." (M. Scott Peck)

- "If you want to make an easy job seem mighty hard, just keep putting off doing it." (Olin Miller)

Procrastinating #11

Personal Experience

When I first set up APLS Group, I thought I had the perfect work schedule planned. Since I was in business for myself, I had the flexibility to have a work life and a home life. I thought my plan was flawless because it allowed me to have a work/life balance.

Monday afternoon I would prepare for all activities for the week (training materials, copies, collating, phone calls, reservations, pack). Tuesday, Wednesday, and Thursday were reserved for working on-site with clients. I planned to complete billing, correspondence, and paperwork on Friday morning, and by noon my work week would come to an end.

Within weeks of opening APLS Group, I found that prospective clients wanted to hire me for training and consulting on Mondays. My business was new and I was hungry for revenue opportunities. As I mentioned earlier, it took four months to get the first paying client. Soon I worked most Mondays and the paperwork began to pile up. I convinced myself that I would finish the paperwork on the weekend, but my family needed me on Saturday and Sunday. Before long, I was inundated with paperwork, overdue billing, and delinquent correspondence. I had to come up with a new plan because "I'll get to it" did not work.

Funny anecdote: I approached a colleague about doing a training session on the subject of procrastination. His reply? "Oh, let's talk about it later." We never did.

Suggestions

- Create a system to manage your business and review its effectiveness periodically.

- Prioritize business tasks daily.

- Find your most productive time and schedule tasks you tend to put off when you have the most energy.

- Break down tasks into bite-size pieces.

- Always have a back-up plan to prepare for emergencies and unexpected occurrences.

- For a free self-test on procrastination, visit the Mind Tools website at www.mindtools.com.

- Need help getting organized? Read Brian Tracy's book *Eat That Frog! 21 Great Ways to Stop Procrastinating and Get More Done in Less Time.*

 Coach Nanci Says:

- Innovation and monitoring your competition are essential successful business strategies.

- Business failure is the ultimate consequence of ignoring the competition.

- By ignoring the competition, you run the risk of being out of date with a product or service.

- Competitive pricing is vital if you intend to stay in business for the long haul.

- Being blind to trends can cost you customers because you won't know what's hot and what's not.

- Business owners need to know what the competition is doing in the areas of packaging, pricing, positioning, and discount rates.

- Return on investment is dependent on you knowing what the customer wants and providing those goods and services.

Ignoring the Competition #12

Personal Experience

APLS Group was approached by a potential client who wanted to open up a food truck to sell organic fare at festivals and craft shows. The client was tired of the corporate rat race and thought that running an organic food truck was a calmer alternative that she and her husband could do together. I encouraged her to check out all the systems that had to be in place for the organic food truck business to become a reality. It was also necessary for the client to take a hard look at the competition.

I guided her through the decision-making process by asking a few preliminary questions: Who was her competition? How would she separate herself from the competition? Was there enough market share at craft shows and festivals to support a business? Did she have a truck equipped for cooking? What type of licenses beyond a business license were involved in opening up a mobile food truck? Fortunately, the client was agreeable to being coached.

After her initial research, the client realized that she had a narrow focus on what it would take to get this business off the ground and profitable. She was going to have to retrofit a kitchen inside a truck. There were competitors doing a similar business and the return on investment would not cover the start-up costs. Her research proved invaluable and kept her and her husband from investing in an idea that would have been costly, with no guarantee of success.

Suggestions

- Knowing your competition can help your business innovate and anticipate customer needs and wants.

- Knowing your competition allows you to differentiate your products and services from others in the same business.

- You can provide the value customers are seeking by building relationships, offering superior service, and fulfilling customer needs better than the competition.

- Talk to and listen to your customers. Remember: feedback is a valuable gift!

- Read *Minitrends: How Innovators & Entrepreneurs Discover & Profit from Business & Technology Trends* by John Vanston and Carrie Vanston

 ## Coach Nanci Says:

- Identify your strengths and passion before you determine your target market.

- Develop a brand that reinforces your vision and credibility.

- Create a detailed marketing plan with both strategy and outcomes.

- Hire (or barter with) an experienced marketing professional to create or review your marketing copy, materials, and plan.

Sloppy of Ineffective Marketing

#13

Personal Experience

When small business clients come to APLS Group for our services, a recurring theme of "doing it all" emerges. Many times we hear that the business does not have enough personnel to do checks and balances for the services they provide. When it comes to marketing your small business, checks and balances of marketing material is a must. The more eyes that see marketing material before it reaches the marketplace, the better.

APLS Group had a client who learned the hard way that marketing mistakes threaten credibility, injure your brand, and negatively affect your bottom line. This small business owner wanted to offer a buy one/get one deal to bring in business, and since she was a one-person shop, she decided to save time by altering an old coupon she had offered in the past. This client did not take into account that the previous product offered in the old coupon was of cheaper quality and yielded a larger return on investment than the item in the current coupon. The price points were drastically different.

The business owner was overwhelmed running her business and juggling multiple projects alone; getting up early and staying up late resulted in mental and physical fatigue. In this compromised state, she undercharged for the product and forgot to include limited-time beginning and ending dates on the coupon.

The client thought she had cut and pasted, spell-checked, and edited the coupon carefully. After sending it out, she immediately started getting calls and walk-in traffic. She wondered why customers were responding so early and thought they had incorrectly read the coupon. When the business owner finally looked more closely at the coupon, she discovered it was her mistake. Instead of increasing sales, she ended up losing revenue because she had to honor the coupon immediately. The length of the sale was much longer than she had originally anticipated, and the pricing error cut into her profit.

Having another set of eyes review the coupon before publication could have saved her from this serious marketing error.

How many of you noticed the heading for this chapter is incorrect? Did you spot the error? (We did that on purpose.)

Suggestions

- Enlist someone to edit your marketing material before you release it to the marketplace.

- Be careful what you say because it cannot be taken back without damaging credibility.

- Incorporate marketing into your business plan year-round.

- Monitor your marketing efforts monthly to check their effectiveness and return on investment.

- Check your local community college for low-cost or free marketing workshops for small business owners.

- Consider hiring a business intern from a local college to help you set up your marketing plan or increase your marketing efforts. Interns often work for college credit or minimal compensation because they want the business experience.

 ## Coach Nanci Says:

- Customer service is the #1 priority of your business.

- Treat your customer as a person, not a policy.

- Listening to your customer can help you anticipate their needs.

- Customer care is no longer a perk; it is demanded because the customer has options.

Ignoring Customers' Needs #14

Personal Experience

One entrepreneur shared a caution-worthy experience with me about an exercise coach who blatantly ignored her needs as a customer. She shared this experience because as a client of APLS Group, she knew we value paying attention to customer needs and exceeding their expectations.

The small business owner signed up to work with an exercise coach at a health club. Initially the coach was personable and attentive to the customer's needs. Within weeks, however, the coach attempted to upsell products and services seemingly without regard to her customer's benefit. The customer questioned the value of the exercise program and asked for more variety, but the coach countered with personal tales of woe and continued upselling. The customer requested a new coach because her needs were not being met.

This experience is indicative of what many customers experience in the marketplace. Customer service practices in businesses that serve the public are inconsistent across industries and among different locations, and their effectiveness largely depends on company culture.

APLS Group advises small business owners to observe how they are treated at businesses that they frequent and duplicate in their own businesses the positive customer service practices that they find.

Suggestions

- Do not patronize your customer. Treat your customer with the same level of service you would like to receive.

- One size does not fit all. Develop a relationship with your customers to help clarify their needs.

- Include friendliness and empathy as the cornerstones of your customer service.

- Interview customers to discover their core needs and expected outcomes.

- Be present and visible to establish an alliance between the business and the customer.

- Encourage repeat business through your customer service approach and create customer loyalty.

 ## Coach Nanci Says:

- Location is a reflection of your business image.

- Seek a professional when selecting an appropriate location for your business.

- Consider traffic flow and convenient access to your customer.

- Determine whether a stand-alone storefront, strip mall, shopping center, mall, or online presence is best for your particular business.

- Based on the type of business, a virtual office may be an option.

Location, Location, Location

#15

Personal Experience

Early in my career, I worked for a non-profit association located in the Washington, DC area. The association's location was convenient for both clients and employees. The commuter train, bus, and taxi service were in close proximity to the building, and a parking lot was in the lower level of the building. A diverse variety of restaurants were located within walking distance from our office.

The association experienced a surge of growth, and the board decided to move the office to another area. The new building had an impressive address in a revitalized area of Virginia where many similar non-profit associations had taken up residence. The office building had functional conference areas and adequate working space for employees, but there were no other businesses around us for any kind of interaction.

Unfortunately, the new building was closer to Reagan National Airport than the vital part of city. The only easy access to transportation was by car or taxi. A free parking lot was adjacent to the building for clients and staff.

Since the association had many business clients, it was essential that restaurants be nearby to accommodate clients for lunch or dinner when they came to the office for meetings. The closest restaurant was located in a neighboring hotel. The only alternative was a salad bar at the local market which was not conducive to business conversation.

The initial location for the association was in the heart of Arlington, VA near the *USA Today* building. It was easily accessible to clients and employees even though it was located in a bank building. The second location, while visually more appealing and spacious, was isolated and inconvenient for the business and social needs of clients and employees.

Suggestions

- Have a clear idea of what location will work best for your business.

- Research demographics of other businesses in the area.

- Examine space for compatibility with local zoning, city ordinances, and regulations.

- Ensure that customers can easily find your location.

- Check foot traffic flow as viable for your business.

- Look for a location with adequate parking.

- Evaluate security in the area for employees, suppliers, and customers.

- Investigate accessibility to the business for vendors and employees.

- Get to know your potential neighbors.

 Coach Nanci Says:

- The need for instant gratification is detrimental to the success of your business.

- Let go of old patterns and beliefs about business ownership that do not include waiting for perks or reinvesting in the business.

- Vision, dedication, commitment, and reinvestment are four keys to operating a sustainable business.

- Outward image is secondary to real success.

- Shift your thinking from instant gratification to delayed gratification to protect the integrity of the relationship between business and customer.

Giving In to Instant Gratification #16

Personal Experience

As a coach, I have seen unrealistic expectations about what it means to be a successful small business owner that often resulted in the demise of many small businesses. I knew a young entrepreneur who opened a small business selling energy drinks to order. Prior to opening the business, the entrepreneur researched the feasibility of profit in the energy drink market overall and in his potential area. He created a business plan; obtained financing from savings, family and friends; and secured a location. He marketed to businesses he had relationships with in his former employment and they agreed to order product from him.

The business opened with a bang. Anticipating the continuation of the opening days' vitality, the owner hired his recently laid-off neighbor at a mid-level manager salary to manage the store. The owner spent his time away from the store courting potential business with long lunches and lavish dinners at expensive restaurants. He drove around town in a recent-model Mercedes. Over time, the owner's image was counter to reality. He enjoyed looking prosperous, but the business was not living up to its original potential.

As time went on, more money was being paid out in rent, equipment rental, salaries, expenses, and marketing than coming in from energy drink sales. The owner added pre-packaged health products to his inventory, but he could not mark them up enough to make a dent in his profit margin. Within a year, the business was on life support. The owner refused to fold, but he was in serious debt with an unprofitable business.

Suggestions

- Resist the temptation to spend before you earn.

- Have a plan for how to disperse profits to support your business.

- Image and visibility are less important to customers than quality, price, and punctuality.

- Shift the paradigm from instant gratification to the core principles of your business and the message you are communicating to your customers.

- Resist the temptation of image as a business motivator.

- Believe in your business plan and trust your idea as the road to success.

- Hire the appropriate people with the skill sets you need at an affordable salary. Compensation can be adjusted as the business progresses.

Coach Nanci Says:

- It is easy to neglect family, friends, or activities in your life when running your own business.

- Isolation can overwhelm a small business owner, causing disconnect between the dream business career and reality.

- Sedentary, isolated pursuits are not conducive to productivity.

- Delegation is a key factor in creating an effective work/life balance.

- Always have an emergency contingency plan for business and personal pursuits.

The Balancing Act

#17

Personal Experience

When I opened APLS Group in 2000 I had not yet created my alter ego, Coach Nanci, but I needed her expertise. As you may remember from chapters seven and eleven, "Attempting to Go It Alone" and "Procrastinating" respectively, I felt confident becoming a small business owner because my skill sets were in order, overhead was low, I had an intact business plan, and I had learned from my mistakes in my previous small business venture.

I had a room set aside in my family home that I shared with my husband, my son, and our dog, Sunny. The room had a desk, a telephone, a computer, and two file cabinets. I thought I had a solid weekly work flow plan, but early on I discovered the loosely-designed routine cross-pollinated home and business activities. My day started with walking the dog and making morning coffee, then I moved on to morning business calls. The afternoon included lunch with or without friends, followed by afternoon mail and calls. Occasionally I watched a television program while throwing in a load of laundry. Late afternoon was time to prepare dinner, have family time, and then get back to the office from 9:00pm to 11:00pm. This schedule went on for months until paying clients interrupted the routine. I had to leave my home/office to train, consult, or coach.

As a small business owner, I had to weigh my options. Leaving my home office meant a shift from having home and office easily accessible to separating the two and developing yet another new routine. I was afraid to incur the costs of adding another expense to a new business, but late nights playing catch-up and writing proposals as a one-woman shop was impeding my ability to move the business forward.

After much deliberation, I reluctantly made the decision to move to an office suite that was equipped with a conference room, secretarial support, and all the amenities of a business office. It was a positive move that allowed me to separate home and business, thereby creating the balance that allowed me to grow APLS Group.

Suggestions

- Make a flexible prospective daily schedule along with your business plan. Revisit and revise as necessary.

- Network with other business owners in and out of your business area.

- Be flexible and lean into discomfort to create balance.

- Include your family and friends in enjoyable activities.

- Incorporate down time into your daily schedule.

- Drop activities that sap energy.

- Delegate business tasks that do not demand your attention.

- Make time for exercise at least four times a week to relieve stress and promote health.

- Meditate daily.

- Home-based business owners should consider reading *The 30 Second Commute: A Non-Fiction Comedy about Writing and Working from Home* by Stephanie Dickison.

Coach Nanci Says:

- Networking allows you to stay current on trends.

- Knowing other business owners in your area can help you accommodate your customers when they need goods/services that you do not offer

- Networking can yield referrals from other small business owners.

- Lack of networking can be attributed to impatience and keeping ideas close to the vest.

- Embrace discomfort and make the effort to interact with other small business owners in your area as a safety measure. You can watch out for each other.

- Allot time to network as part of your balancing act because the interaction can lead to new business and social connections.

Ignoring the Importance of Networking

#18

Personal Experience

Years ago when my family and I moved to North Carolina, I worked in a company for five years where my position required extensive weekly travel. I was unaware of the career value of networking and did not consider myself stationary enough to pursue it in or out of the business. It was not until I got laid off and came into contact with an outplacement service that I learned the benefits of networking. Based on the counselor's suggestions, I began joining professional associations, volunteering, and going to monthly meetings for trainers and consultants. Eventually I was recruited to be on the board of a professional association. Networking helped me to meet people, market my skills, look for my next career opportunity, and create an effective 30-second elevator speech. When I opened APLS Group, networking proved to be a valuable tool that helped move the business from idea to incubation to success.

When the recession came in 2008, small businesses were hit especially hard. Companies postponed training and limited the use of outside consultants. I watched colleagues who previously shunned networking either go out of business or dust off their resumes to apply for temporary full-time positions. Networking helped me weather the recession by partnering with other trainers and consultants to deliver services and receive referrals for other training opportunities.

Suggestions

- Develop a support group of individuals both professional (labor, capital, raw materials) and personal (friends, family).

- Use social media to ease into networking via LinkedIn, Facebook, Twitter, and Pinterest.

- Join industry associations at national and local levels.

- Build alliances with other business owners and vendors in your area.

- When networking, remember to ask how you can help the other person.

- Genuine sharing of ideas often produces referrals and positive bottom-line results.

References

Chapter 1

Horan, J. (2015). *The one page business plan for the creative entrepreneur*. Berkeley, CA: The One Page Business Plan Company.

Chapter 2

Kamaroff, B. (2013). *Small time operator: How to start your business, keep your books, pay your taxes and stay out of trouble*. Lantham, MD: Taylor Trade Publishing.

Chapter 5

Horan, J., & Monosoff, T. (2010). *The one page business plan for women in business*. Berkeley, CA: The One Page Business Plan Company.

Scarborough, N., Zimmerer, T., & Wilson, D. (2011). *Effective small business management*. New York, NY: Pearson.

Chapter 6

Higham, William. (2009). *The next big thing: Spotting and forecasting consumer trends for profit*. Philadelphia, PA: Kogan Page.

Chapter 7

Carol S. Dweck. (2007). *Mindset: The new psychology of success*. New York, NY: Ballantine Books.

Chapter 10

Seashore, E., Seashore, C., & Weinberg, G. (1997). *What did you say? The art of giving and receiving feedback*. Columbia, MD: Bingham House Books.

Stone, D., & Heen, S. (2015). *Thanks for the feedback: The science and art of receiving feedback well*. New York, NY: Penguin Books.

Chapter 11

Tracy, Brian. (2007). *Eat that frog! 21 great ways to stop procrastinating and get more done in less time*. San Francisco, CA: Berrett-Koehler Publishers

Chapter 12

Vanston, John. H, & Vanston, C. (2011) Minitrends: How innovators & entrepreneurs discover & profit from business & technology trends. Austin, TX: Technology Futures, Inc.

Chapter 17

Dickison, S. (2009). *The 30 second commute*: A non-fiction comedy about writing and working from home. Toronto, ON: ECW Press

www.aplsgroup.com

For additional copies of this book or to see Nanci's other books, please visit:

https://squareup.com/store/aplsmarketplace

Interested in having Nanci speak at your event? Please contact Joy Drew at joy@aplsgroup.com or 919.424.6339.

Made in the USA
Middletown, DE
21 April 2018